# Voices from the West:

## Life Along the Trail

### by Katharine Emsden

© Discovery Enterprises, Ltd.
Lowell, Massachusetts
1992

© Discovery Enterprises, Ltd., Lowell, MA 1992

ISBN 1-878668-18-8 paperback edition
Library of Congress Catalog Card Number 92-74781

10   9   8   7   6   5   4   3   2

*Printed in the United States of America*

*Subject Reference Guide:*
Westward Journey
Oregon Trail
Santa Fe Trail
Gold Rush – California Trail

## Photo Credits

The photograph and illustrations in this book are from the Denver Public Library, Western History Department, Denver, Colorado.

## Acknowledgments

For their help in providing new information, I thank Dale Watts of The Kansas State Historical Society and Jim Horn of Bent's Fort.

For enabling me to attend the Myth and Reality Institute, I am grateful to The Colorado Endowment For The Humanities.

For their encouragement to present a more representative picture of the West for young students, I thank University of Colorado History Professors, Gary Holthaus and Patricia Limerick.

## Dedication

*In memory of my father, James Mount Nicely, whose great great grandfather travelled west through the Cumberland Gap to Indiana Territory. Throughout his life he valued justice, friendship, and world peace over economic or personal prestige.*

# Table of Contents

# Foreword

When was the last time you travelled? Perhaps you have vivid memories of moving to another state or of flying over mountains or oceans to reach new places. Did you take photos, send a postcard, or keep a journal? If so, you have created the raw materials of history, for history is nothing more than the collected memories of what happened when people came together.

How do you happen to live in America? Perhaps your ancestors lived here for as long as anyone can remember. Perhaps they came from Spain with Juan de Oñate in 1600 and raised sheep in the Southwest long before it became part of the United States. Did your forefathers sail to New England during the Colonial times? Maybe your great great grandfather and grandmother were among the 500,000 who travelled to the West in covered wagons between 1840 and 1865. Their journey is the subject of this book.

When a large group moved into land that was already occupied there were often conflicts. Those who ended up in control celebrated their success in songs, news reports, paintings, victory dances, and books. Records from the same time events took place are called primary sources. This book contains pages from three pioneer diaries, daily observations along western trails. Susan Magoffin and Helen Buckingham were eighteen years old when they wrote their journals. Susan married shortly before she departed for Santa Fe, which was then part of Mexico. Helen went with her aunt and uncle to Oregon Territory. William Clark left his family temporarily to join the Gold Rush in Sacramento, California, which had just become part of the United States. These eye-witness accounts provide us with personal impressions.

Historians study primary sources from a certain period to tell us their views of what really happened and why, who made it happen and how it influenced people's attitudes. Their books and essays are secondary sources. The three essays in this book give background information and enlarge the picture to speak for Native Americans, African Americans, Hispanics, and others whose stories need to be told for a fuller understanding of our past.

The longer poems were written within the last few years. In her poem, "Thirst," L.A. Fleming shows how a child might have felt while crossing the plains. Gary Holthaus has created an entire history of western North America in poetry. His book, entitled *Circling Back*, portrays the West as a meeting ground of groups who crossed the Bering Straits from Asia and immigrants who came from Europe much later. In these excerpts, he takes on different voices: Indian chiefs, buffalo, and the land itself.

If you had travelled the trails you would have passed through the homelands of many tribes. You would have had experiences none of your friends back home could even imagine: buffalo herds stretching to the horizon; a thunder storm enveloping the world. Next morning the hay bales were soaked so you fed the ox team the straw from your mattress! It's all there, in the diaries and poems, which you can now read for yourselves.

# Thirst

## by L.A. Fleming

*"Oh, it is beautiful, lots of cattle and wagons moving and behind us and ourselves moving on in the general throng, the sand reflecting back the heat of the sun on your face and making the sweat trickle down. Oh, this is going to Oregon!*

— diary entry of eighteen-year-old Helen Marie Stewart, 1853

Dry passage:
oxen pulling wagons
loll out their tongues.
Shoes of hide are tied around
their hooves, sore
on baked ground. A girl
climbs down from a wagon,
every step a lurch,
it keeps moving;
she's tired, brushes dusty hair
from her face, smiles.
Ahead in the train
rides her father
perhaps a brother
ahead of the line, itching
to race on to Oregon.
Who knows where
they are, except somewhere
slow and hot
on the way, where at night
water takes a long time
to boil. Few tracks are found.
The great salt lake
was weeks ago. She knows
the dark ridge on the horizon
means more mountains.
The sky rests pale and empty,
heavy against the back

of the trail. A lizard
watching the parched train
from his warm rock has never
seen a running brook.
Sweat salt in her mouth, the
girl knows not to lick
her lips, already shredded,
throbbing as they peel
and crack like the trail.
She thinks about the bath
she will take when she gets
to Oregon, how she'll wash
her hair and rinse it, pouring
just-drawn water onto
her scalp, watching it pool
where it drips off
her bowed head. She imagines
ice caught under her tongue
and sucks at her mouth.
Until the train finds water,
she will drink a cup a day
like all the rest. It is enough
to get her where she's going.
She pulls her skirt up as she
walks, as oxen pull the train
inexorably on, as she and
forty families dream and
march, thirsty, to Oregon.

# Mexican Silver Along the Santa Fe Trail

After 1492, when Christopher Columbus claimed the Americas for the new Spanish crown, Conquistadores and missionaries were able to bring tribes and land under their control north to Oregon and east to the Mississippi River. Coronado took an expedition to Kansas. Father Escalante rode or walked 1200 miles along The Old Spanish Trail between Santa Fe and Los Angeles. Our major Californian and New Mexican cities today bear the names of early Spanish missions.

After wars in Europe gave France the central third of North America, President Jefferson bought it from Napoleon by The Louisiana Purchase of 1802. He immediately sent Meriwether Lewis and William Clark, with the help of Sacagawea and York, to find a water route to the Pacific Ocean. He also sent Lieutenant Zebulon Pike to survey the new southern boundary at the Red River of Texas. The West had become U.S. property by the stroke of a pen, and the major trails to the Northwest and to the South were mapped in three short years.

Pike's book was an inspiration to Americans who wanted to trade their goods for Mexican silver coins. Many people had lost all their money due to bank closings.* Settlers along the Missouri were lured by tales of an elegant culture in Santa Fe. Then in 1821, Mexico had its own War of Independence from Spain, and suddenly needed goods from another source.

It was perfect timing. William Becknell was a ferry operator on the verge of bankruptcy, and he was willing

* See Notes p. 56 - 57.

to take any risk. As soon as Mexican Independence was declared, he started across the 900 desolate miles to Santa Fe with three small wagons and twelve men. Four months later he returned to Franklin, Missouri and showered silver coins on the pavement! He had just become "the father of the Santa Fe Trail," as it says on a marker today. The following year, he took three Conestoga wagons filled with 5,000 pounds of calico and building materials, and returned to Santa Fe.*

The Franklin newspaper reported highlights of his journey: buffalo "pies" made excellent fuel for cooking when wood was not available; prairie dogs tasted awful; wild horses and buffalo filled the Arkansas plain.

In Santa Fe, the Mexican Governor welcomed Becknell. He found that the Spanish-speaking descendants of settlers brought by Oñate in 1598, had frequently intermarried with Indians, yet were still very class conscious. The very poor served the very rich, and life was much less democratic than in the United States. In Susan's diary, one Senora uses a servant as a footstool!

Fifteen years later, Becknell, Josiah Gregg, and other Yankee traders were collecting a total of a million dollars worth of silver reales each year. Mexicans began to bring their wagons and extra mules to Independence, Missouri in order to buy wholesale and because they did not have to pay as high an import tax when bringing goods back to Santa Fe. Everyone profited, and for several years you could have heard as much Spanish spoken in Independence as English. Missourians drove Mexican mules and wore colorful serapes or Indian blankets. Navajo women today continue to weave the thoughts of their ancestors into beautiful designs out of wool from Spanish sheep.

Three brothers built Bent's Fort as a resting place along the Santa Fe Trail. Kit Carson hunted game for the traders who stopped there. Sioux often visited to buy flintsteel and tin boxes for storing embers. Inside the adobe walls of the fort, traders could press beaver pelts to allow a greater load and profit when they sold them in St. Louis for eight times the price they paid.

Wagons cost $500, mules $75, and oxen $25 with extra for the yoke. An average Conestoga needed six to eight mules. Traders dressed in their best frock coats signifying that they were the elite. On the banks of the Missouri River the travellers elected a captain to make important decisions for the wagon train. He checked the water barrels and had the tar buckets filled to caulk the wagon slats before crossing the river. He made the choice of campsites, judged how far to go each day, and watched for danger. His word was law.

Susan Magoffin, eighteen and newly married to Samuel, an experienced trader, started for Mexico in 1846. Susan came from a wealthy Kentucky family and was the first woman to travel the Santa Fe Trail. She had the luxury of a private carriage. Samuel was one of ten children in an Irish immigrant family.

The Magoffins took fourteen wagons with six yokes apiece, two riding horses, eleven mules, and two hundred oxen, who threatened to turn around as they started. That evening a Kaw Indian trader passed by, bringing skins from Bent's Fort. He was invited to their first camp-site supper, and Susan wrote in her diary that he was fascinated by the white man's way of cooking. The first night in her tent she was bitten by mosquitoes, heard wolves, and met her first grasshopper, which she called "an alligator in miniature."

Susan mentions thousands of buffalo close by. She met a Comanche Chief who spoke both English and Spanish. One hundred miles later someone died of tuberculosis, and the oxen helped stamp the earth over his grave. Susan became very sick after drinking from a pool of sulphur water. Her carriage proved not to have been such a good idea. It tipped over a cliff, and her husband risked his life to pull her out from underneath. At Bent's Fort she watched a Pueblo woman give birth and then carry her baby to the Arkansas River to wash it off. Susan's journal for that day pokes fun at all the fuss her people make over having a baby; she says it probably weakens the mother. Unfortunately, Susan herself had a miscarriage while at the Fort.

The diary which Susan Magoffin wrote in 1846, at age eighteen, gives us a rare glimpse into her thoughts and times. You can read more in her own words, written as she left Santa Fe and went further south to Chihuahua.

*Note:* The diary excerpts in this book have been reprinted as they were originally written, with misspellings, some archaic expressions, and some creative use of grammar.

# Diary of Susan Shelby Magoffin
## October 7 – 23, 1846

*Wednesday 7th. Camp No. 1. El rancho de Delgado.*
We are camping again! and after all it is quite as good
as staying in Santa Fe. I was impatient to leave. Gabriel
[Valdez] and William [Magoffin] are with us now. The
wagons are all on ahead, and we'll not reach them yet
for some days. Left Santa Fe about 12 o'k. came on fifteen miles to this place—a little farm, called a rancho
—rather a poor place, only a little corn, beans, and
an abundance of *chile verde* [green pepper], a few goats,
sheep and jacks—the beast of all work—they pack wood
on them, ride them, take all their little "fixings" to market
in baskets or bags swung on the long-eared animals
back &c &c. We camped pretty near the house and of
course the peepers are not a few.

The women stand around with their faces awfully
painted, some with red which shines like greese, and
others are daubed over with flour-paste . . . .

*Friday 9th.* The boys have been out all day with their
guns trying to shoot grullas (sand hill crains) which a-
bound here in the river bottom, feeding off the rancho
cornfields—but they returned to be laughed at only—
They shot, each, some eight or ten times only, and good
sights too, but all were fruitless.

. . .We have much pulling through sand and we stop
earlier tonight, on the bank of the Rio del Norte—it
resembles the Mississippi much, muddy and dark, the
banks are low, with no trees—we are buying wood
every day—a small arm-full for *un real.*

A parcel of Indians are around the tent peeping in at me and expressing their opinions. It is a novel sight for them. These are the Pueblos or descendants of the original inhabitants—the principal cultivators of the soil—supplying the Mexican inhabitants with fruits, vegetables &c.

*Saturday 10th.* In passing through a little town this A. M. called Sandia, *my* Indian friend—the one who called to see me once in Santa Fe—who lives there, the big man—head chief among the tribe, stoped the carriage and pressed us to get out and go into his house—he had been expecting and preparing for us. We had no time for this though—and only accepted some grapes at the carriage—he with his family, squaw & children saw us eat them, with pleased faces, and after a little compensation we left them.

Report comes to us that Brother James has been robbed of *all* his things, carriage, mules, trunk, clothes &c. &c. by the Apache Indians and escaped with his life only—how he escaped is a miracle to us. In robbing they always want the *scalps*, the principal part of the business.

I hope it is all a falsehood—though every person we meet confirms it. The last we heard he was in the little town at the Pass of the Del Norte—without a hat.

We have fine grulla today—our hunters have better luck today. They are tender and nice after being boiled nearly all night—the meat is black as pea fowls.

*Sunday 11th.* Started out on a little walk this morning, but it was cut short by the little sand burrs sticking to my feet and dress till I was entirely unable to walk; they are quite a sharp and hurt as much as briers. I

stoped and called for Jane to come to my assistance—
after a long time she succeeded in picking them out.
My fingers are sore now with the little thorns.

Passing through one of the little towns, Alba-
querque we stoped for a few moments at the store
of Don Raphel Armijo, which notwithstanding the
Sabbath was opened.

While they were counting some money *mi alma*
[husband] was receiving. I steped in to take a look at
the premises. The building is very spacious, with wide
portals in front. Inside is the patio, the store occupy-
ing a long room on the street—and the only one that
I was in. This is filled with all kinds of little fixings,
dry goods, groceries, hard-ware &c.

Over took Brother James's wagons this P. M.

*Monday 12th.* Stoped to noon it today for the first
time since we started. The pulling has been altogether
through sand & of course the animals are quite fatigued,
and after a hard pull of two miles through entire sand,
they fare much better to stop. Our resting place is on
the river bank opposite to an Indian village on the other
side, and the warriors and squaws are coming over in
flocks to see the wonderful objects of curiosity—They
bring things to sell—eggs, sandias, tortillas, grapes and
the like. They wish to trade for bottles instead of money.
They readily give *four bits a piece* for an empty bottle,
making a fine proffit for the owners. We can buy in
the States the filled bottles for three or four dollars a
dozen, drink the liquor, and then sell the empty bottles
for six dollars per doz. They peep into the carriage at
me, and talk among themselves, and are altogether

curious in their inquiries of how some things about the carriage and my clothes are made...

*Tuesday 13th*...The house is very large—the sala measuring some—feet. This is well furnished with handsome Brussles carpet, crimson worsted curtains, with gilded rings and cornice, white marble slab pier tables —hair and crimson worsted chairs, chandelebras. And all the Mexicans have the greatest passion for framed pictures and looking-glasses. In this room of Chavez's house are eight or ten gilt-framed mirrors all around the wall. Around the patio are chambers, store-room, kitchen and others. All is exceedingly neat and clean...

We had more squaws to see us this morning—they came trading with *tortillas; cebollas* [onions] watermelons, and *manzanas* [apples]. Bottles are their great passion, and especially thick black ones. One old woman took a fancy to me, and so we got to trading. *Mi alma* told her he did not want her to have it, (in a joke only) but I made him give it, it pleased her so much she called me "*comadre*" [godmother] all the time, and on separating we parted almost like old friends. She *presented* me with some tortillas. I warrant if I should see her ten years hence she would recollect her "*Comadre*" and the *black bottle*. We hear that Calafornia has been taken by Com. Stockton....

*Wednesday 14th.* In our travel today we have met many Indians with their backs loaded with *muchas cosas a vender* [many things to sell]. They fill their *serapes*—[Mexican shawls or wraps for men] with whatever it may be, and start off in the trot natural to the Indian....

15

*Thursday 15th.* Came up with our wagons today at Noon. All is going smoothly. Nooned it near the River, and as usual had some of the country people to see us. We are kept constantly supplied with eggs and small fruits. The apples all seem to be of one kind, and are not good, having a sickening sweet taste and very tough.

*An early photo shows typical horse-drawn wagons along the trail.*

I have opened a regular *mantua* makers [dressmaker's] shop on the Plains. I am sewing on a dress every day at noon and will soon finish it. And I must not wear it out before I get home either—for I wish them to see that I have been doing some thing else than roll along idly in the carriage. . . .Came up with Mr. Harmony's wagons this P. M.

*Saturday 17th.* Left our last night's camp this morning, came only about a mile, over an ugly hill and sandy road—this side found a place for the animals and stoped for the whole day. "as we are in no hurry." There is a little town near to us and we are living on the fine Mexican *tortillas*—and they are fine indeed they are. . .

*Sunday 18th.* This day has been passed at the same camping place of yesterday, resting the animals for a long pull we are to have in a few days without water—a hard drive. . .

*Friday 23rd.* . . . I've made the good graces of another old comadre this morning—an old half Indian, half Mexican—she came in soon after we stretched the tent, and sat a good long half hour or more. We talked of all family concerns from the children down to the dogs. She asked if I had mother, father &c. and said I had run off from them "*just for a husband*," but I laughed and said "*peres es mejor nos*" [Well, is it not better], and with a hearty laugh she assented both to this and my other little question "*el marido es todo del mundo a los mujeres*" [the husband is the whole world to women]. She thinks though I am *young*, I am old enough. . .

*Saturday 24th.* I've had a real tramp this morning through the mud, sliping down the River bank, jumping the *scequia* [acequia—ditch or canal], which last, by the way, is quite a feat—and in fine doing all sorts of wonders of the kind. It has been my desire through curiosity only to get onto a sand-bar in the River, so soon after breakfast, notwithstanding the wet grounds from last night's heavy rain, I put on my rubbers and sallied forth. The first adventure was a long slide down the slippy bank of the saquia—completely mired. . . .

Note: The Magoffins made several trips between Independence and Santa Fe over the next nine years. At age 27, Susan died of yellow fever.

17

# Families on the Oregon Trail

Back in the overcrowded cities of the East, newspapers advertised the new lands of opportunity obtained by The Louisiana Purchase. Citizens over 21 who were willing to cultivate farmland for five years could claim 160 acres! What better way to escape the gray clouds of factory life and grow up with the country? One journalist announced that it was America's "Manifest Destiny" to extend to the Bering Straits, the Pacific Ocean and the isthmus of Panama. Civilization was moving West!

The land race was on, and Oregon became the first destination. Lewis and Clark had shown the way across barren plains and mountain passes to the fertile Willamette Valley. For 200 years the wide Missouri River had separated the new European settlers from hundreds of tribes and trappers who travelled the paths according to the seasons.

In all the history that took place along these trails, none ever again matched the spirit of cooperation at the annual Rendezvous in the 1830's and '40's, before the White man thought of living west of the great river.* Frenchmen from Canada followed in the footsteps of Marquette and LaSalle; English, Irish, Scots, and Russians worked for the Hudson Bay Company in the Northwest; and Americans, including the former slaves, Jim Beckwourth and George Bonga, became experienced guides for the Rocky Mountain Fur Company. George married into the Potowatomi tribe, and Jim into the Crow nation, and both became tribal chiefs. By travois or portage they brought furs to the Green River, where they traded and celebrated with many Indian friends every autumn.

With the first land act in 1842 and because of the new steam-powered boats, the Missouri became a gateway to vast territories of beaver, buffalo, and Native Americans.* Pioneers set off to tame the wilderness and start a new life. They gathered their families, cows, a hoe, and some seed bags, along with provisions for the first year, and departed from their past.

> Fifty thousand persons in an endless
> Train, says Hulbert,
> Travelers and fellow travelers
> Rarely out of sight
> Of one another,
> > "The ratio being 16 men
> > to one woman and three women
> > to every child."
>
> And trudging with them
> 36,000 oxen, 18,000 horses,
> 7000 mules and milch cows,
> And 2000 sheep,
>
> All bent on crossing
> My lively prairie,
> Leaving scars
> Like stretch marks on my belly,
> Cutting a swath through buffalo
> And elk, all the fair game;
> Cutting me open at last
> For gold or grain,
> The people streaming

19

Into this new land,
Recreating the life

They thought they'd left behind...

— excerpt from *Circling Back*,
"West of the Missouri," p. 73.

Narcissa Whitman was the first to choose to go to the Oregon Territory. In 1836, when she was nineteen, she made it a condition of her marriage to Marcus that he take her West to introduce the Cayuse to the Bible. Against her family's wishes, they set out with seven small wagons before the trail had been officially opened.

She describes the caravan as a moving village. For 2,000 miles and four months, nine people went through mud, scorching heat, treacherous mountain ledges, and the roaring Columbia River. When an axle broke, Marcus turned the wagon into a two-wheeled pushcart; when that fell apart, they finished the last 200 miles on horseback. An Indian guide saved their party at the final river crossing, and Narcissa was able to give birth to a daughter several months later.

Soon after the Whitman mission, The Great Migration began. Although it was usually the men who decided to go, the women prepared the wagons, a crucial step in determining the success or failure of the journey. Mothers and daughters sewed shirts and dresses, aprons and sunbonnets, during their last winter in the East. They bought extra bolts of gingham, packed blankets and consulted guidebooks listing what each emigrant needed: 200 pounds of flour, 150 pounds of bacon, 20 pounds of sugar, and 10 pounds each of salt and coffee. Each family needed a cooking kettle, fry pan, pot and cutlery, needle and thread, mirrors and trinkets to trade for buffalo meat. A tent, shotgun, and the family Bible would fit beneath the floorboard or hang from the canvas ceiling. Medicine for the "summer complaint" meant castor oil and peppermint essence. A cookstove, tools, and seed potatoes completed the bare necessities; too many keepsakes might overburden the ox team and have to be discarded along the way. Travellers were always hopeful that someone in the train had brought along a fiddle. Courage, imagination, and a willingness to help were vital to the group's future.

*"Pilgrims on the Plains," by Theo R. Davis, depicts a camp circle of wagons, with the men trying to avert a stampede.*

On the outside of this miniature house on wheels, a pail of tar hung ready to caulk the sideboards at river crossings. Another pail could churn milk into butter as

21

the wagon rocked! A mattress filled with straw, horse-hair, air or water lined the main compartment for those who preferred sleeping in, rather than under, the wagon. A "plunder box" was conveniently placed with items of daily use. Early trailblazers had to rely on logic and then be clever enough to adapt to any circumstances. No convenience stores lay up ahead, and there was no turning back.

Wagons from Independence followed the Santa Fe trail for the first fifty miles and then were floated across the Kansas River before continuing along the north side of the Platte. During the spring run-off of the Rockies, the Platte River was often a mile wide, and yet it was always shallow enough to ford. The nearby path, created by buffalo and Indians, was the longest, easiest stretch of any overland trail. Mormons said it was "carved by the finger of God." Each diary describes the landmarks: Chimney Rock, Courthouse Rock, Scott's Bluff, and Independence Rock, where thousands were to scratch their names with a stone or buffalo bone.

The prairie was an eternity of space and changing skies. Weather played tricks. Phantom rain would pour in sheets that drifted toward earth and then suddenly evaporated. Static electricity could bounce off the horns of cattle and start a stampede. There was a dryness unknown in the East. Even the snow was drier here; it took 100 inches to melt into one inch of rain! Wooden wheels might shrink loose from their iron rims unless taken off and soaked overnight in the river to swell back to normal size. Thick lumps of oil oozed from the sandy soil and provided lubrication for the axles when the train stopped for nooning. No one imagined the oil fields that lay beneath the trail.

For days the Rocky Mountains loomed up ahead, their dark silhouette concealing height and distance. Sweetwater Creek at the base of South Pass often necessitated attaching ropes on a pulley between trees on both sides. Women and children had to unload the wagons while the men swam with the oxen and then combined teams to stand on the far bank and pull the floating wagons over deep water. Herds of cattle followed, sometimes emerging far downstream. Often, during the first twenty years of migration, Sioux and Cheyenne from a nearby village came to help.

Pulleys, ropes, and chains guided the heavier wagons over steep crests, and a log or spare wagon tongue slowed the dangerous descent. It was not unusual for an entire load to tip over a narrow ledge and be lost forever. Early migration families walked rather than ride in a wagon without brakes or springs.

Adequate water became the major problem after leaving the Rockies. Both boys and girls would help fill the barrels as they came upon a clear spring. In desperate thirst, livestock often headed for poisonous or alkali pools, and everyone rushed to drive them safely past. Cholera, yellow fever, or smallpox took lives on almost every large wagon train.

Children had more than their share of accidents. Small boys liked to ride up front on the wagon tongues, and in a sudden lurch they could be crushed to death beneath the wheels. A stampede of buffalo or frightened cattle caused parents to grab their children in terror.

When arguments broke out and a lone wagon left the train, there was a risk of invading Indian lands and being the target of a raid. A few women and children were captured by Indians, usually in retaliation of a broken treaty or out of anger at watching their own children forced to follow the White man's ways on reservations. The captives might be traded or later rescued. Some chose to stay. Accounts of kidnapped children, such as Jane Wilson, became the subject of popular novels, and every family feared the "Redskins," although most never saw any at all on their journey West.*

Sundays provided a day of rest, especially for the animals. Women caught up on their washing or aired the flour and baked a tubful of bread for the following week. After doing their share of gathering wood, children explored, held contests, and made friendships among the other families. For everyone, Sundays were a welcome break in the routine.

However we may wish to have been part of pioneer history, many a young bride or mother must have felt moments when tedious work and loneliness were overwhelming. Martha Farnsworth's diary tells of leaving late in the season and being caught in a blizzard. She travelled over snowy plains for weeks without seeing a living thing. "It was a journey so hard that many times I lie on the mattress behind Johnny and cry my heart out and he thinks I'm sleeping. Women will sacrifice everything for the man she loves." (*Plains Woman: The Diary of M.F., 1882-1922*, Ed. Marlene & Haskell Springer, Indians UP, Bloomington 1986, p. 85.)

In 1850, '52 and '57, an almost unbroken line of 45,000 covered wagons rolled along the Oregon Trail each year from April to August, "like a great white serpent through a sea of green grass." A sort of prairie post office developed; strips of cloth or paper were pinned to trees, rocks, buffalo bones, and even human skulls! "Stewart Party took Sublette Cut-Off, June 10, 1853." "Water here is poison. We lost 6 of our cattle." In 1850, one sign on a Sierra pine tree read: "President Zachary Taylor has died." News was so scarce that some emigrants arrived at their new home without realizing that the area had just become the latest State in the Union.

One of the many romances along the trail comes down to us from such notes. In 1851, John Lawrence Johnson took a liking to 16 year old Jane Jones. Her father, a minister, disapproved and found an excuse to leave the other wagons in the train. Just before they were separated, the couple discovered his plan and made a plot of their own. Whoever was ahead would write a note each day, leave it on a buffalo skull, and use the pseudonym, "Laurie." When John and Jane met up a month later, not a day had passed without Jane finding a note from "Laurie." It told her how far ahead he was, and she predicted when her train would overtake his wagon. John's diary ends before he reached Oregon, and so we can only guess the story's ending.

The Dalles, flat rocks beneath the Columbia River rapids, was the final hazard before entering the Willamette Valley. For some, like George Washington Bush, ex-slave and fur trapper, it was the start of a new challenge. The provisional Oregon government had put "whites only" at the head of its list of rules. The rest of his group was furious and refused to claim their settlements until the Bush family was allowed to join them. For travellers, arrival meant new freedom from past hardship. Some suffered more than others. Native Americans suffered the most.

This unending straight line of settlers invading their ancient homeland circles of life-giving resources threatened the existence of every tribe. Forced removal to less desireable sections of land so that newcomers could exercise their rights of cultivation and ownership was the unwritten tragedy of Western history. When a chief complained of treaties broken or ignored by the Bureau of Indian Affairs, he was told that, as a non-citizen, he was not allowed legal rights. In many ways the Oregon Trail became the trial scene for 800,000 Native Americans, and just as a jury might incarcerate one criminal, they were convicted and sentenced to reservations. Even today, few Indians can live near the sacred sites of their ancestors.

When this part of our history was being made, Harriet Talcott Buckingham wrote her own account.

# The Diary of Harriet Talcott Buckingham
## May 4 – September 23, 1851

[Document B]

*May 4*  Crossed the Missouri at Council Bluffs, where we had been a couple of weeks making the final preparations on this outskirt of civilization.

*"Kanesville – Missouri River Crossing – 1856," a watercolor painting by William Henry Jackson, who crossed the plains in 1866.*

The weather has been mild, and we have walked evry day over the rolling hills around – one day found a young physician and his wife who were interested in examining the numerous skulls and human bones that were found near the surface of the ground. After much speculation the fact was elucidated that, large tribes of Indians from the middle states had been pushed off by our government to this frontier region to make room for white settlers, and had here perished in large numbers by starvation consequent upon removal from familiar hunting grounds: they had been buried in large trenches with heads to the east. Skulls were thick: of peculiar shape differeing from the Anglo Saxon type.

We number seven wagons – one carriage, a large band of oxen & cows, horses & mules – the latter are for the carriage – oxen for the wagons. Mrs Smith myself and a little girl occupy the carriage – we have a driver – Mr Smith rides a little black mule that is very intelligent & a pet with him.

There are drivers for the wagons and loose stock. Mr E. N. Cooke & family have a nice carriage & about the same equipment. Mr Hiram Smith has crossed the plains twice before & so knows how to do it  Mr Smith & Cooke travel together intending to go by the way of Salt Lake City for the purpose of selling to the Mormons Goods & Groceries with which most of the wagons are loaded so we make quite a cavalcade as we slowly move along. We have tents & small cook stoves.

Mr & Mrs Smith have had the carriage so arranged that a bed can be made of the seats, & when the curtains are all buttoned down there is a comfitable sleeping apartment  The little girl & I sleep in one of the big covered ox wagons in which is a nice bed – really makes a cosy little low roffed room, it has a double cover – Mr Smith has a coop fastened on behind the carriage which contains some fine white chickens – three hens and a rooster. We let them out evry time we camp, and already they seem to know when preperations are made for moving & will fly up to their place in the coop. Mr & Mrs Cooke have a niece Miss Brewster, & a little daughter, an uncle & a young gentlman Mr T. McF Patton, with them, so we have a nice little society of our own.

*May 5*   We are now travelling through the country of the Omaha Indians. They demand toll for passing so Mr Smith promises them a feast, & they have sent sumners [summoners?] out to bring in all the tribe who are not already out Buffalo hunting

*[May] 6''*   Hosts of the Indians have arrived on Indians Ponies. Squaws & little Pappooses – young men in the glory of fine feathrs paint & skins – their war costume, for they are just now about to go to fight the Pawnees. The girls who are in the market are most grotesqely painted in vermillion & Green – they have not yet assumed the cast off garments of white people –

The Calf which Mr Smith & Cooke gave them was killed and eaten even to the very entrails, some hard Bread was given to them too.

In the evening they gave us a war dance by an immense fire, that lit up the wiered [wierd] hob goblin scene – their fiendish yells, as they tossed their arms about and swung the gory scalps just taken from their enemis, the Sioux: helped to give the whole affair an informal aspect. . . .

*11 May*   The Platte river is beutiful here – many islands dot the stream & are covered with cotton wood trees –

We ladies went to visit some Indian Graves near here & were piloted by Mr Patton. Some of the graves were larger than others, all were mounds from five to six feet in highth. Earth & stones heaped up in a conical shape

The Indians were so hungry & persistent – They levy tribute on all who pass – do not always get anything – but it is wise to do as they will stampede the cattle some dark night if not well treated...

*Tuesday May [13]* We were quickly wakened this morning by the singing of the Indians. Our men all went to work with the three other companies building a bridge. It was completed by afternoon when we crossed. It is a matter of surprise that over 500 head of cattle, & fifty wagons should cross without accident The Waggons were all drawn over by hand & the cattle & horses swam. This day was pleasant we encamped a mile from the creek The Evening was delightful the moon shone so Clearly but before morning, it clouded up & one of the most terrifine storms I ever witnessed. The heavens seemed to be opened The rain fell in torrents The lightning was most vivid. We were obliged to move as soon as possible for fear of being overflown Our cattle was skatered miles around us. they were not together till nine Oclock when we traveled on some 3 miles in water up to the axeltrees. The 13 & 14 of May will long be remembered by this bunch of Oregonians. . . .

*June 1* . . .The Pararie is covered with beautiful little flowers. Whose fragrance surpassed any garden flowers. There is a modest little white flower which peeps up among the green grass. Which particularly strikes my fancy. I call it the Pararie Flower Autumn sun will bring the more gorgeous flowers

*June 2* . . .At about noon we passed Ancient Bluff ruins. Mr & Mrs Cook, Sue, Tom, Joe & I climbed the highest ruin which commanded a fine view of the country.

This is of Solid Rock with five scraggy gnarled cedars, Throwing their twisted arms over the over-hanging precapice  Many a name was carved with knife upon the bark  We left our names upon a Buffalo bone which lay bleaching upon the top from the river it presents the appearance of a fortified city falling to decay, but the nearer you draw nigh the illusion vanishes. . . .

*June 3*  . . .Today an antelope stood close by the road side so that I could see it quite distinctly it was a beautiful little creature. It gazed at us for a moment & then bounded away to the Bluffs. . . .

*June 5*  . . .Camped upon the Platt  our vision was delighted with the view of a few small trees that grew upon the banks for they tell strongly of good cheer after having to cook so long with Buffalo Chips  For 200 miles we have no wood. Bluffs are not so high on the south – more sandy, rainy & unpleasant.

*June 6*  Started early road by the first of the day over level plains  Nooned upon Raw Hide Creek  In the afternoon passed three companies, travel rocky, passed the fort in front of which was a Sioux village of some hundred Lodges & great numbers of ponies. The squaws were just herding them in as we passed. . . .

*August 3*  We came 13 miles & camped upon the Weber with the boys who were herding cattle. Our eyes were once more greeted with our old friends Sage & Sand, whose acquaintance we had formed in the black hills Our road lay through a pass in the mountains to a by place some distance from the main road. scenery wild & grand. O for a lodge in some vast wilderness, a home in some deep lone "kenyon"  We were under the brow of the mountain by the side of a cool spring. There were

two of these, one they had used to wash dishes in &
dress fish – the other for drinking for they had dammed
it up to form a basin allowing the water to run from
one side – we went further up the kenyon in search of
Raspberries not finding any. Sue & I took off our shoes,
& walked upon the shallow pebly bottom of the noisy
Weber while Mrs S & C sat upon the bank trying to
frighten us with stories of snakes & toads. To day again
we thought to try our fortune in berrying  some of the
young gentlemen of the camp went with us & taking
each a pail & basket of hard bread & venison we
started invoking the gods to be more propiteous for it
was a long toilsome walk to climb the Rocky Mountan
& then not to get one raspberry it was too bad though
we did find wild currants & service berries but we were
a merrie party. O it was so hard to climb – to jump from
rock to rock sometimes swinging ourselves by holding
a shrub & clinging to the roots  after ascending about
a mile, we heard the tricling of water & pushing the
bushes by my side found a small spring where the water
was dropping from between the stones  we held a cup
under & were quite refreshed with a drink of ice water
Two miles brought us to the long sought berries – O
my poor hands – mess – but never will our dinner [be]
finished & pails filled in a short time. I never saw larger
ones cultivated in our gardens at home both white &
black but now came the tug of war for we were to come
down again....as we came down upon the bottom we
met two of our men panting & out of breath, with their
guns  They had seen two Indians on the opposite side
& they had shot at them, and hurrying to camp got
their guns & came in search of us. We hastened home

but I will confess that I cast a suspicious glance behind every big rock or thicket. . . .

[August] 6   Today two Utah indians visited our camp with skins & service berries to "swap" weather delightful though rather windy at sunset lasting until the rising of the sun. our cattle number 203 horses & mules d[itt]o.

[August] 7   Today we camped upon a small creek beyond Fort Ogden  This is a settlement which is rapidly improving, situated upon the west side of Ogden river a beautiful stream of clean cold mountain water. There has been two Indian burials not far from our camp  The last was the Chiefs brother. He was wrapped in skins tied around him with Lariets & laid upon a horse. He was carried up into the mountans followed by the whole tribe who were howling & screaming most hideously. . . .

[August] 15   Last night about midnight were awakened by the sudden tramping of the cattle who were herded in the correll. Indians! Stampede! before two moments elapsed all hands stood ready to fire  imagine to yourself forty men rising like specters from under waggons tents & carriages with guns & bowie knives – cattle, scattering with speed & the bright moon rising over our heads & then form a faint idea of the consternation & chagrin that momentarily depicted itself upon their countenances – when the guard said it was he who accidentally frightened them causing this small stampede  soon all were gathered in the correll  Then the laughter & merry jests –Then all was quiet again. . . .

[August] 18   Travelled over sage plains, roads rocky and dusty Rocks sharp and hard. Bear River vally is the most inhabitable looking since we left the Platt

The Crickets are large often an inch and a half or two inches in length – Black & shiney, the Indians make soup of them – They catch them by driving them into pits dug for this purpose – they are dried for winter use, its laughable to see our White Chickens try to swallow them, it often takes two or three efforts to get one disposed of, they are so numerous that one cannot avoid stepping on them. . . .

[August] 21 . . . Numbers of *Shoshone* Indians are camped here, We brought enough Salmon of them for a fish hook to make us wish never to see any more. The Fish is poor by the time it gets this far from the ocean. The falls prevent them going farther, so the water at certain seasons are alive with them, some of enormous lengths – as long as a wagon bd [bed]

Our road is often through light sand ten inches in depth – which is hard on cattle – whose feet are now very tender.

[August] 22 We crossed snake river to an Island & then to a second Island, where was nice grass, with plenty of wood & water. Here we missed some Horses & the tracks showed that they had been run off by Indians at Ft Hall. Volunteers went back under the control of Mr Cooke so as to get to the Indian camp before sunrise that they might be taken by surprise, & so be able to capture the Horses. The camp sorrowfully watched the departure of our warriors, & a sleepless night followed – After twenty-four hours of anxiety the absnt ones were seen returning with all the missing stock.

They reported the consternation of the Indians at the appearance of hostile whites. The squaws & Papposes took to the hills for refuge & were seen issuing from evry Lodge. The men half dressed with bow in hand stood at bay ready to repel intruders. But viewing the rifles pointed at them folded their arms and awaited events. Mr Cook gave them by signs to understand that he wanted Horses  they signified that they had none,  after some more strategy one seized a Lariet & soon returned with the missing stock  Mr Cooke recovred his old favorite "Barnabas" with delight, so ended the battle of "Wagon Hill". . . .

[September] 8  . . .Came down the mountain into Grand Ronde vally – a perfect gem – an oasis in a desert  The descent was made with difficulty – the wagons being chained & let down with ropes much of the way. . . .

Thousands of horses – many of them curiously spotted feed upon the mountain side. Hundreds of Indians of the Nez Percies tribe, are camped here, & lazily greet us with invitations to swap, saw one child almost if not quite white among them. The women are all dressed in native costumes of dressed antelope skins – fringed & ornamented with moccasins on their dainty little feet. They came to see us mounted astride of great sleek horses, & laugh & chatter among themselves like just so many gay school girls. Their long black hair is braided into two long plaits that hang down & top of the head is a gay little hat shaped like a flower pot – made of woven grass – it serves to pick berries in or to drink out of, as it holds water it being so closely woven. Brass rings are to be seen on waist & ankle  they have an air of maidenly reserve that wins respect. The men are all fine specimens of physical development, & have not yet become contaminated with the vices of white men and the whole tribe are very superior to any we have yet seen. One pretty squaw took my knitting & very proudly took a few stitchs – the remains of some of the teachings of Mrs Whitman that had been remembered

Grass was tall & luxuriant in this Indian Paradise.

[September] 15  Crossed the Dechutes river – very rocky & difficult. We were told the story of an emigrant woman who was afraid to cross with her train, but was persuaded to get on a horse behind an Indian that had just crossed. When in the middle of the stream with dizzy brain she cried out in fear. The Indian turned his face to her & said, "Wicked woman put your trust in God" These words in good English frightened her worse then ever – He was one of Whitmans good Indians & he had been taught this by that missinary martyr

[September] 23  found us at the Dalles of the Columbia. Most of the train went on crossing the Cascades mountins & the rest of us came by boat & raft to the Portage of the Cascade, where we camped. The little steam boat James G Flint brought us part of the way

Indians were salmon fishing at the Portage & were drying their fish there. They had a great dance dressed in costume – none but the young men danced. The occasion that called for it reminded me of some of the customs of the ancient Iseralites and I wondered if indeed, they were of the lost Tribes of Iseral.

Many fine canoes were to be seen, made of great length out of trunks of great cedar trees – some might be fifty feet in length hollowed out & carved with high sculptured prows, glistning with brass headed nails & it was wonderful to see the skill with which they would handle them. The squaws all seemed to be rich in ornaments of beads & brass strings of beads of all colors weighing pounds hang from the neck, – all looked happy and contented  sevral Indian burial places we passed as we walked from one end of the portage to the other. . . .

*26 of sept*   we landed at Portland a little town of a couple hundred inhabitants, just as the guns were booming in honor of the completion of the Plank Road to Taulatin plains. . . .

## Nuggets, Haloes, and Sweet Chariots:
## Hitching Wagons to Other Stars

Gold was discovered in the Sacramento Valley the same year the United States gained California from Mexico. The largest single group of Americans set off, most of the time less interested in settling than in getting rich quick and returning to families in the East. They were less careful in making preparations, and many risked unknown short-cuts when they left the Oregon Trail west of the Rockies. Those who travelled in 1849 encountered the worst summer weather of any year.

The Donner party split off through the Sierra Mountains, ignoring the advice of Indian guides. A few survived only because they lived off the flesh of mules and humans who perished in an early autumn storm. A twelve-year-old girl in the group summed up the trip with a warning: "Never take no cut-offs and hury along as fast as you can."

The spring of '49 was uncommonly cold. At Independence, one man slept forty nights in his wagon, waiting for the grass to sprout enough to feed his mules along the way. Leaving too late meant risking blizzards at the other end. Chilling winds and bitter nights continued across the plains all summer. Flour and sugar were ruined by rain, wheels sunk to their hubs in mud, and cattle ran for miles during hailstorms and a Nebraskan tornado in May. Many people died of cholera. Teamsters had to wear kerchiefs over their faces to avoid the pain of whirling sand and gravel. The Forty-Niners had the roughest experience of any along the trail. Some chose to reach the California goldfields by steamer. It was more expensive but safer and faster. At times they had to burn the furniture to keep the engines moving, and those who went overland through the isthmus of Panama risked yellow fever and malaria for the promise of instant wealth.

Relations between miners and Indians worsened. Isolated skirmishes made headlines, and myths of racial superiority became policies of extermination. When the Federal Government spent $80,000 to open a shorter route from Sioux City to the mines of Virginia City, local Crow warriors retaliated at the destruction of their homelands. By a treaty in 1865 they gave up the 300,000 square miles promised them in a treaty signed fourteen years earlier. The Crow were "removed" to the north, and soon the Northern Cheyenne and Nez Perce were forced from their ancestral homes because of gold discoveries there. Unfortunately, the Chinese who found employment in the mines were also mistreated.

Former slaves, emancipated after the Civil War, looked to the West to live out their new freedom. President Lincoln had originally intended to release them to another country for the same reasons that the Indian Removal Act put Native Americans out of the White settlers' way. However, thousands of black pioneers joined together and founded settlements in the West.

After gaining his freedom, an ex-slave, Uncle Harrison, stayed on to serve his mistress. When she died he discovered she had willed her plantation to his family, but he was quickly dispossessed of it by her heirs. Penniless, he and his wife joined an expedition to Virginia City, Nevada, and were welcomed there.

Two other former slaves organized The Exodusters, which helped thousands of African Americans settle in towns such as Nicodemus, Kansas.

Others took to the cattle trails, becoming the majority of cowboys who drove ten million steers north from Texas within the next twenty years. Deadwood Dick worked the Chisholm Trail to Abilene, leading 25,000 head of cattle through floods, poisonous weeds, bandits, and the remaining Indian territory. Using the Big Dipper as a "clock," other cowboys followed the Goodnight Trail to Canada, crossing rapids and fighting off wolves. Mexican partners showed them how to use wide-brimmed hats to fan the embers, carry water, or ward off a charging steer. They would often put a ball of bees wax inside as protection against lightning! Many expressions grew up along the cattle trails. "Mavericks" were unbranded cows, "G.T.T." meant that you'd "gone to Texas" so that a sheriff couldn't find you, and "well-heeled" indicated that you wore Spanish inlaid spurs. Longhorns were another legacy from the cargo of the Conquistadors.

Intent upon religious freedom for the Mormons, Brigham Young* led the first church wagon trains to the Great Salt Lake. During the 1860's three thousand Mormon emigrants arrived annually, pushing handcarts 1500 miles across the plains. They saw an opportunity to run ferry services and mercantiles for the gold seekers and other travellers.

The Mormon Companies were tightly organized trains of 100 families. Each had ten hand carts, one yoke, two milk cows, and a tent. One pioneer to Salt Lake, Appleton Harman, invented a roadometer which, when mounted on a wagon wheel of sixty cogs and

*F.R. Grist, "Crossing the Platte, Mouth of Deer Creek"—*
*a calmer crossing than many.*

activated by a screw, would measure the mileage. Sometimes a simple scarf was tied on, and a child would count the revolutions as he or she walked. The diaries carefully record daily mileage. The Mormons showed special skills in using western herbs for tea and saleratus for baking soda. Some went on to northern New Mexico, but the majority, including 16,000 Europeans, stayed to build Salt Lake City.

> Who cares to go with the wagons?
> Not we who are free and strong!
> Our faith and arms, with a right good will
> Shall pull our carts along.

> (Kreyche, p. 24)

Another unusual vehicle created for western trails was the windwagon. Mr. Thomas outfitted a wagon with two sails and completed a 200 mile roundtrip on the Santa Fe Trail. Later, the Rocky Mountain News, April 18, 1860, reported that three men had arrived in Denver from eastern Kansas after twenty days on a windwagon. They claimed it was as fast as a horse team at one-tenth the cost. In three hours it travelled fifty miles and passed 625 teams. An Indian challenged this "white man's bird" to a race and grinned when he lost. Because it depended on wind alone, it could never fulfill the inventor's dreams of carrying mail and freight.

The Pony Express, however, did operate a mail service for sixteen months beginning in 1861. Riders carried 35,000 letters, wrapped in oiled silk, over the 1,966 miles between St. Joseph and Sacramento. They galloped in ten mile relays, covered the one-way trip in ten days, and charged up to $10.00 per letter.

In the same year, the Civil War started, and both Union and Confederate soldiers marched along the wagon trails to forts and to battles. When the war ended, many soldiers received land in the West as pay, and a new surge of emigrants left the East. With the completion of the Trans-Continental Railroad, fewer people crossed in wagons. Stagecoaches and eventually our own "horseless carriages" transformed trails into highways.

John Hawkins Clark must have added soul and spirit to his travelling companions. In 1852, he took the Oregon Trail, stopped to see the famous Brigham Young, and then headed for gold.

# Excerpts from John Hawkins Clark Diary
## May 6 - September 4, 1852

*John Hawkins Clark travelled the Oregon-California Trail to Sacramento in 1852. He stopped in Salt Lake City in July of 1852, during his journey to California.*

*The following excerpts from his diary, entitled, "Overland to the Gold Fields," express his admiration for the Mormons and their leader.*

*May 6.*—. . .There are many musicians belonging to the different encampments surrounding us, and after supper all commenced to practice the sweet tunes that were to enliven us while sitting around the camp fire on the far off plains. . . . This concert lasted until near midnight, when all was hushed except the crackling of the log fires. . . . Many and varied were the feelings I experienced on this the first night of my pilgrimage in the wilderness I was about to encounter. Sleep at length came to rescue me from uneasy thoughts of home, wife, children and friends.

*May 7.*—It took [nearly] all day to put up our wagons, adjust the harness, break the oxen, store away our provisions in the different vehicles of transportation, count out the cooks, drivers and train master. . . . About six miles from camp to the high lands through a wilderness of woods, mud and water. After a hard day's work through mud knee deep we pitched our tents upon high land near a spring of good water and wood in abundance. . . .

*May 8.*—Bright was the morning and light our hearts as we rolled out of camp on this, our first day's journey of 2,000 miles. . . . As far as the eye can reach the road is filled with an anxious crowd, all in a hurry. Turned out at twelve o'clock to let our teams to grass, which was quite abundant all along the line of our day's travel. One o'clock we are again on the move. . . . Camped at six o'clock; wood and water to carry some distance, but plenty of good grass.

*May 9.*—An early start this morning over a good but hilly road. . . . Our progress was stopped to-day by a small stream spanned by a small bridge. Here was not the d———l to pay, but instead a large Indian sat at the receipt of customs demanding $1 per wagon for the privilege of crossing over. California should be full of gold if the immigrant expects to get back all his outlay in getting there. . . . We presented a $5 gold piece but it was refused; he must have "white money with the bird on it," so eight silver half dollars were hunted up and we passed over. The Indian was making a good thing, "not less than 1,500 wagons passing over to-day. . . ."

*May 10.*—Saw the first dead ox on the road to-day, and passed two or three graves, the occupants of which, it is said, died of smallpox. Met a young man with two small children returning to the states; said he had buried his wife and one child just beyond. We felt for the poor fellow as he every now and then turned his look toward the wilderness where lay his beloved ones. . . .

*May 14.*—Camped last night on the bank of the Nemaha river, and this morning were called upon to bury a man who had died of cholera during the night.

There have been many cases of this disease, or something very much like it; whatever it may be it has killed many persons on this road already. . . .

*May 22.*—Being in the Indian territory we keep a sharp look-out for our stock. A good many cattle have been stolen lately. . . .

*May 25.*—Rolled out very early this morning to make the Platte valley. . . . At ten o'clock we are in the bottoms of the Platte. . . . The water of the Platte, like the Missouri, is thick with sand which gives to it a muddy appearance, forbidding to the look, nevertheless good and sweet water; it is thought to be more healthy than water found in springs along the line of travel. Many immigrants were camped on the shores of this river, many busied themselves fishing, hunting, running and jumping, playing cards and dancing. . . .

*May 29.*—We were determined to hunt good camping ground for to-night and also for the morrow, as it is very necessary that we should lay by on the Sabbath day. There are many things to attend to; washing is once in awhile to be done; our firearms need brushing up and there are a variety of little things to look after; one has some little gift from someone at home and it must be seen to; another a Bible which is stowed away somewhere. The most of us have little pictures of our sweethearts and wives. . . .

This was quite a warm day and we and our teams suffered much from the heat. Camped near the river; good grass and plenty of water, of course, but no wood. This was about the first time we could get no wood. Wood or its substitute we must have; there is no getting along without coffee on these plains. We had read . . .

that people traveling over these plains had "sometimes to use buffalo chips," and it took us but a little while to come to that conclusion ourselves. We gathered them by the basketful. . . The "chips" worked like a charm and are really a godsend for the traveler in this part of the country—a staple which would be hard to dispense with. . . . The inquiry when camp is announced is whether or no there is "plenty of chips." If there is we can stay, but if not we must move a little farther on. . . .

*June 12.*—. . .Fort Laramie is a great place in the immigration season; a good many wagons are left at this point, many coming to the conclusion of getting along without them. . . . A hotel, store and post-office are located here. I saw about 150 officers and men belonging to the Fort; all appeared to be well behaved, and I think ready and willing to help the unfortunate. . . .

We are now at the head of the great open valley of the Platte river. If this stream was only navigable what a smoking there would be in the great valley. . . . Could only console ourselves with the pleasant expectation of one day seeing the "iron horse" on his race with time go thundering up this great highway on his course to the Pacific. . . .

*June 14.*—Remained in camp to-day to shoe our horses and fix up things generally. . . .

At dinner we were visited by a party of native Americans, and as they were on a mission of peace added greatly to the pleasures of camp life. . . . We immigrants had been so long on the plains and lived so much like Indians that now, while sitting round the camp fire, passing the pipe from mouth to mouth, from white man to Indian, a stranger would have sworn we were all of the same tribe as we smoked together. . . .

*June 18.*—The sublime, the pathetic, the outrageous and the ridiculous follow each other in quick succession on this road. This morning while in advance of our train caught up with an old lady trudging along after her two wagons. "Well, how are you getting along?" I asked. "O, terrible bad," she replied; "one of my grandchildren fell out of the wagon yesterday and both wheels ran plum over his head; oh dear! I shall never forget yesterday!" Thinking the accident a painful one for the old lady I changed the subject; in the meanwhile several little fellows that were in the wagon were making a fuss, climbing up on the side boards, swinging to the roof of the cover, and otherwise disporting themselves. The old lady ever on the watch called out to "Johnny" to behave himself. "Do you want to fall out again and be killed, Johnny?" "Is that the boy who got run over yesterday? I thought he surely must have been killed." "No, it did not quite kill him, but it made the little rascal holler awfully." I thought that boy's head must have been a very hard one; or, possibly there might have been a very soft spot on the road somewhere. I asked the old lady if the children fell out of the wagon often. "They fall out behind sometimes when the wagons are going up steep places, but that don't matter much you know, for then there are no wheels to run over them," she replied. . . .

*June 23.*—. . .From this point to the topmost heights of the Rocky Mountains is our next stage of travel. . . . The road becomes crooked, rough and flinty; the face of the country a broken mass of natural ruins. . . .

This is the land of the mirage, of "delusions," of the sage brush, and the alkali waters; a land of wonders and of hardships; a land to be avoided or left behind as soon as possible. Saw many dead cattle on the road; the poisonous water and the great scarcity of feed begins to tell on the poor brutes. . . .

*June 25.—*. . .The great rock lies just before us and we were eager to get upon its back. . . . The view from this elevation is a very extensive one. . . .

*Devil's Gate, an important landmark on the trail to Salt Lake, as painted by William Henry Jackson.*

Do you see yon huge range of mountains some four or five miles to the west? Well, do you see that it is split asunder from the bottom to the top, a narrow and perpendicular opening of some 400 feet through solid granite rock? That little opening is called the "Devil's Gate." By looking very closely at the bottom of that opening you can discern a little silvery thread of water

48

issuing from it. . . . I hardly know of a more interesting spot than that on the top of Rock Independence. . . .

*July 4.*—The mosquitos are so bad that we are obliged to leave our last night's encampment—leave the good grass, the tall timber and the grateful shade. It is the 4th of July and we expected to remain in camp and "celebrate." Our college friend had promised an oration, but. . .the mosquito holds the fort and we are obliged to retire. . . .

*July 13.*—Seven miles yet to the city of the Mormons, five of which we are to travel through a deep, dark canon whose walls are hundreds of feet in nearly perpendicular height. . . . Eight o'clock and we are on the borders of the great valley. Quarantine ground lies at the gate of this canon and here is a hospital, or what pretends to be one, established by Governor [Brigham] Young, where all, both great and small, Jew or Gentile, are obliged to report. . . .

This should be a pleasant and desirable country to live in and in time will be densely populated. The Mormons are, I am told, extending their settlements through the country and in time will make it a flourishing part of the world. . . . The Mormons are ridiculed and disliked by many, yet they are good to their kind. When it has been known that companies of Mormons were in destitute circumstances. . .their brethren were ever ready to send out men and teams to bring them in when all hope by their own exertions had failed.

It is admitted by all that Mormons are a brave people; indeed, any people who can leave a civilized country. . .and journey hundreds of miles over an almost unknown country. . .to have a peaceful home can honestly claim to be brave people. If these people should continue to prosper as they have in the past they will soon become great. . . . Many of these people are now comparatively wealthy–fine farms, well stocked with horses, cattle and pretty women. . . .

As I was on a visiting tour among the neighbors, I called at a house where three women belonged to one man. These women were all young and had children. The father of this young brood is a yankee from the state of Maine. . . . Being a shrewd kind of a fellow he had located a farm in this neighborhood and, as he told me, was trying the experiment of building up a farm and raising a family. He has now a good farm well improved, and well stocked with cattle; three wives and nine children and not a soul on the place over twenty-seven years of age. If this "experiment" is not a success, I do not think it is his fault. . . .

Went this morning to mail my letter and to see the city and Brigham Young. The city is quite an ordinary looking place; may compare with the country towns of Illinois and Indiana. . . . My desire was to see the great man, Brigham Young. . . . I had not long to wait; he came out of a business house and stopped on the side-walk with some friends long enough for me to see that with age, he had grown stouter and broader and his hair more gray, otherwise he appeared to be but little changed.

Brigham Young is a king among men; smart as the smartest; ambitious as a politician, bold, daring and aggressive; unscrupulous and tyrannical; born to command and he has made the most of his abilities and his opportunities. His word is law to these people and they obey without a murmur. No other man perhaps could have led them so far from civilization and planted them so happily in this far-off, beautiful and fertile valley. . . . Without him they would be lost. . . .

I have learned that the government intends to regulate the matrimonial affairs of this people. If the attempt is made, heroic measures will have to be resorted to. These people will fight like Turks rather than give up the religious privilege of keeping many wives. The church has encouraged the institution and almost made it a sacred duty for man to take as many wives as he can possibly accommodate. . . .

*Aug. 18.*—To-day we make the last grand effort of this wearisome trip; this is considered the hardest bit of travel on the route, and consequently more preparation is made for the journey. We have grass and water on board for our teams which is now universally carried, the distance about forty miles. . . . About ten miles out the dead teams of '49 and '50 were seen scattered here and there upon the road. Very soon, however, they became more frequent and in a little while filled the entire roadside; mostly oxen, here and there a horse and once in a while a mule. Wagons, wagon irons, ox chains, harnes, rifles and indeed all the paraphernalia of an emigrant's "outfit" lay scattered along this notorious route, reminding one of the defeat of some great army. . . .

*Aug. 23.*—Crossed the [Carson] river for the second time and put up for noon in a shady grove and beside the swift running stream. . . . Chinamen were mining for gold at this place; they told us they were making four to six dollars per day to the man. We did not believe the story. Here is also a trading post where vegetables, canned fruits, bacon, flour, mining implements and bad whiskey are kept for sale. . . .

*Sept. 1.*—Left camp early; road good but very dusty. At four o'clock we caught sight of the city of Placerville; at five we put up at the Ohio House. . . . We are now in the center of the mining district. . . .

*Sept.4.*—. . .To our left stands Sutter's Fort, an ancient and dilapidated-looking concern, all gone, or going to decay. . . . How earnestly did we gaze at the sight of civilization; from the first of May to the first of September we had been wandering in the wilderness; everything we heard or saw appeared new. . . . At 12 o'clock we entered the city of Sacramento, dirty, dusty and hungry, our teams and ourselves worn down with fatigue and looking for all the world like the remnant of a disorganized army that had just escaped destruction.

# Epilogue

The reality of entering the wilderness was harsher than the dream. Yet within an amazingly short time half a million pioneers chose the trail of Western opportunity, where what you did was more important than who you were or where you came from. It took courage and hard work to start from scratch, cooperation and willingness to adapt to new surroundings.

Reading about The Great Migration we become more aware of the Native American and Spanish cultures which were already here and which are, once again, playing a greater role in communities throughout the United States today. When the White Man began to farm the lands of the buffalo, he did not always think of the consequences of his acts. Overgrazing and single-crop planting turned much of the West into a Dustbowl. Any Indian could have told us so.

> We knew the White traders and trappers well.
> We learned their ways and had many dealings
> With those explorers who would bring others.
> We were kind to them,
> And honest in our way.
> They were only a few and we did not mind,
> But they became many and intolerable.
> Betrayal was their way
> Even when they loved us.
> They did not know what they were doing
> Nor did we
> Until it was too late.

— excerpt from, "We Are All Related,"
*Circling Back*, p. 31.

I have been hunted with fire
And survived;
Surrounded, driven over ledges
Struck by arrows, by darts
By lances and by lead
And survived.
My real dangers were
Wagons, railroads,
Fences and ploughs.

— excerpt from, "Litany of the Buffalo,"
*Circling Back*, p. 90.


"Over pieces of land they are wrangling
Over iron and oil and fat lands,
Over breed and kin and race pride. . .
And the little wars are leading on
into the big war to come.".

Watch this conflict with me,
See our agreements broken,
The bonds loosed, cut or torn,
The words unravelling like cobwebs curling
Above the terrible orange perimeter
Under the smoke.

"Neither fear nor courage saves us,"

— excerpt from, "Prairie Fire,"
*Circling Back*, p.145.


In the words of Albert Jerome Dickson, written
after he arrived in Oregon and watched Chief Joseph's
Nez Perce tribe greet the pioneers with a tribal dance:

"Nothing was intelligible to the white visitors except the spirit of good will prevailing. His qualities of leadership were only equalled by his capacity for friendship. All who knew him loved him. Every inch an Indian, he was every inch a man." (*Covered Wagon Days: A journey across the plains in the sixties, and pioneer days in the NW; from the private journals of AJD*, p. 221, 225, UNebP, 1989).

If we who took over the land had known the significance of these dances, if we had thought to learn languages we encountered and then sat in a council circle, the land might have responded better to our sharing. Like Columbus, our nation was wrapped up in its own beliefs and ambitions. Let us hope we are learning to respect the land and people we meet along the trail that leads us into the future. We are all related, we are all one.

> Perhaps we'll find
> A better word
> And in some future now,
> If there are any of either of us,
> Perhaps we'll come
> To some new term
> And try once more
> To build a word between us
> And start anew –
> What's left of me,
> What's left of you –
>
> Agreed?

— excerpt from,
"Litany of the Buffalo,"
*Circling Back*, p. 102.

# Notes

*Bank closings* (p. 8): In 1837 there was a prolonged Depression. President Jackson had said that banks were a monopoly of the rich. When he refused to let banks issue bank notes, and insisted everything be paid in gold or silver, many people went bankrupt, banks closed, and 200,000 people lost their jobs. Paper money became almost worthless, and there was a desperate need for hard currency, such as Mexican silver.

*Conestoga Wagon* (p. 9): Originally made in Pennsylvania, these huge wagons could carry 5,000 pounds and required ten mules to pull them. They worked best on flat trails and were used for the first years of the Santa Fe Trail. Merchants preferred them because the import tax was the same for all wagons, and the Conestoga was the most profitable because of its great capacity. Teamsters, often smoking "Stogies," operated the wagons and skillfully managed the oxen. They would crack whips over the ox's head without touching it. By 1859, one freighting firm had 6,000 teamsters and 45,000 oxen for hire. A wise teamster lashed on an extra wagon tongue, the board from the front axle to the harness.

*Rendezvous* (p. 18): Up to 2,000 trappers and Indian families gathered annually along the tributaries of the Missouri or at the Green River west of the Rockies. Kit Carson was often there. Trappers filled their "Possibles" bags with blankets, beads, axes, and kettles, in exchange for guns, powder, bullets, traps, knives, and horses. Feasts, races, and story-swapping lasted several weeks.

Today, several Mountain Men Clubs hold Rendezvous in the Rockies.

*Land Acts* (p. 19): The Pre-Emption Law of 1842 stated that whoever cultivated 160 acres could buy them at a minimum price. The more far-reaching Homestead Act, signed by President Lincoln in 1862, enabled anyone over 21 to gain title for up to 160 acres of surveyed land provided they had improved it during five years' residence and could pay a register fee of $1.25 per acre. In 1873, homesteaders were allowed another 160 acres if they put one-quarter of it into trees. By 1880, 1,500,000 land grants had been issued.

*Indian Encounters* (p. 24): Tribes respected one another and offered tribute gifts when entering each other's territory. Stray horses were fair game for whomever found them. Thus, when wagons came through a tribal homeland without tribute, the Indians considered them intruders. It is worth noting that in the skirmishes, often over live-stock, more Indians were killed than whites. The later massacres, ordered by a few Generals, often without provocation, decimated several Native American tribes.

*Brigham Young* (p. 50): After Mormon founder Joseph Smith was captured with his followers in Illinois, Brigham Young became the Mormon Governor who led 85,000 people to the isolated regions of Salt Lake. Six thousand of them died along the way. Young has been described as a king among men, determined to represent the Mormon Community as morally, mentally, and physically enter-prising.

# A Selected Bibliography

*Book Links: Connecting Books, Libraries, and Classrooms.* Chicago: American Library Association: Booklist Publications. July, 1992.

Brown, Joseph Epes. *The Spiritual Legacy of the American Indian.* Pendle Hill Pamphlet, No. 135, 9th Printing. Wallingford, 1983.

Brown, Sharon. "What the Covered Wagon Covered." *Overland Journal*, Vol. 4, No. 3 (1986): 32-39.

Katz, William L. *The Black West.* Seattle: Ethrac Publications, Inc., 1987.

Kreyche, Gerald F. *Visions of the American West.* Lexington: University of Kentucky, 1989.

Limerick, Patricia Nelson, Clyde A. Milner II, Charles E. Rankin, ed. *Trails: Toward A New Western History.* Lawrence: University Press of Kansas, 1991.

Limerick, Patricia Nelson. *The Legacy of Conquest: The Unbroken Past of the American West.* New York: W.W. Norton, 1987.

Schlissel, Lillian. *Women's Diaries of the Westward Journey.* New York: Schocken Books, 1982.

Unruh, John D., Jr. *The Plains Across: The Overland Emigrants and the Trans-Mississippi West.* Champaign: University of Illinois Press, 1979.

Weber, David J. "The Spanish Legacy in North America and the Historical Imagination." *Myth and Reality: The Legacy of 1492.* Teacher Institute, sponsored by the Colorado Endowment for the Humanities and Adams State College. Alamosa: 1992.

# Further Reading for Students

## Includes Primary Sources:

Blumberg, Rhoda. *The Great American Gold Rush.* New York: MacMillan Bradbury, 1989.

Buckingham, H.T. "Crossing the Plains in 1851," *Covered Wagon Women: Diaries and Letters from the Western Trails, 1840-1890.* V. III. 9 Vol. Kenneth L. Holmes, Ed. Glendale, CA: The Arthur B. Clarke Company, 1989.

Clark, John Hawkins. *Overland to the Gold Fields of California in 1852.* Ed. Louise Barry. *Kansas Historical Quarterly,* XI, August, 1942, 227-296 (used by permission of the Kansas State Historical Society).

Fisher, Leonard Everett. *The Oregon Trail.* New York: Holiday, 1992.

Holthaus, Gary H. *Circling Back.* Salt Lake City: Gibbs M. Smith, Inc. Peregrine Smith Books, 1984.

Magoffin, Susan S. *Down the Santa Fe Trail and into Mexico: The Diary of Susan Shelby Magoffin, 1846-1847.* Stella M. Drumm, ed. Lincoln: University of Nebraska Press, 1926.

Meltzer, Milton. *The Chinese Americans: A History in Their Own Words.* New York: Harper Collins, 1980.

Richmond, Robert W., Robert W. Mardock, ed. *A Nation Moving West: Readings in the History of the American Frontier.* 2nd Printing. Lincoln: University of Nebraska Press, 1967.

Smith, Carter, ed. *The Conquest of the West: A Sourcebook on the American West.* Fresno: Millbrook, 1992.

Wexler, Sanford. *Westward Expansion: An Eyewitness History.* New York: Facts on File, Inc., 1991.

## Secondary Sources:

Katz, William. *Black People Who Made the Old West.* New York: Harper Collins, 1977.

Lasky, Kathryn. *Beyond the Divide.* New York: MacMillan, 1983.

Simmons, Marc. *Ranchers, Ramblers and Renegades: True Tales of Territorial New Mexico.* Santa Fe: Ancient City Press, 1984.

Thomasma, Kenneth. *Kunu: Escape on the Missouri.* Jackson, WY: Grandview, 1989.

Westridge Young Writers Workshop. *Kids Explore America's Hispanic Heritage.* Santa Fe: John Muir Publications, 1992.

## About the Author

Katharine Nicely Emsden has a B.A. in History from Swarthmore College and an M.A. in English from the University of Denver. She taught for many years in Colorado and is now at the Shady Hill School in Cambridge, Massachusetts. With her three children she has camped in the West and in Europe. While living in Colorado she directed a pilot program for autistic children, taught a creative writing course at Canon City Prison, worked as staff reporter for *The Douglas County News Press*, and arranged for 5th graders to tape interviews with pioneer families.

Her winning essay was published in *2010: How Peace Came to the World*, MIT, 1985. A poem, "Testimony," appears in *Poems of Great America*, v. 2, National Arts Society, 1989. Recently, a trip to the Ute homelands in the San Luis Valley proved as important as the more traditional research which went into writing *Voices*.